Day and Night

Crystal Sikkens

CRABTREE
PUBLISHING COMPANY
WWW.CRABTREEBOOKS.COM

Title-Specific Learning Objectives:

Readers will:

- Identify information in diagrams, pictures, and in the text, and explain how visuals support understanding.
- Recognize that Earth's rotation causes daytime and nighttime, and that they repeat in a cycle.
- Observe and compare features of the sky during the day and night.

High-frequency words (grade one)	Academic vocabulary
and, away, day, get, is, it, look, make, our, the, to	cycle, diagram, directly, Earth, Moon, observe, pattern, repeat, senses, telescope

Before, During, and After Reading Prompts:

Activate Prior Knowledge and Make Predictions:

Have children read the title and look at the cover images. Ask children:

- What do you think this book will be about?
- How are the pictures on the front cover different? How are they similar?

During Reading:

After reading page 7, stop and ask children:

- What is the main idea on this page? Explain the idea in your own words.
- Why does the text say that the Sun "seems" to move across the sky? (Encourage children to refer to the pictures and captions in their answers.)

- How do the pictures and captions help us understand the main idea on the page? (Encourage children to notice the position of the Sun in each picture and make comparisons.)

After Reading:

Have children take one day to individually complete the Venn diagram on page 21. Come back together as a group and encourage children to share the observations they made. Discuss the ways each diagram was similar and different. Create a class Venn diagram on an anchor chart. Incorporate all of the shared observations that were discussed.

Author: Crystal Sikkens

Series Development: Reagan Miller

Editor: Janine Deschenes

Proofreader: Melissa Boyce

STEAM Notes for Educators: Reagan Miller and Janine Deschenes

Guided Reading Leveling: Publishing Solutions Group

Cover, Interior Design, and Prepress: Samara Parent

Photo research: Janine Deschenes

Production coordinator: Katherine Berti

Photographs:
All photographs by Shutterstock

Library and Archives Canada Cataloguing in Publication

Title: Day and night / Crystal Sikkens.
Names: Sikkens, Crystal, author.
Description: Series statement: Full STEAM ahead! | Includes index.
Identifiers: Canadiana (print) 20189061472 |
  Canadiana (ebook) 20189061480 |
  ISBN 9780778761877 (hardcover) |
  ISBN 9780778762348 (softcover) |
  ISBN 9781427122537 (HTML)
Subjects: LCSH: Day— Juvenile literature. | LCSH: Night—Juvenile literature. | LCSH: Sun—Juvenile literature. | LCSH: Moon—Juvenile literature. | LCSH: Sky—Juvenile literature. | LCSH: Astronomy—Juvenile literature.
Classification: LCC QB521.5 S55 2019 | DDC j523.3—dc23

Library of Congress Cataloging-in-Publication Data

Names: Sikkens, Crystal, author.
Title: Day and night / Crystal Sikkens.
Description: New York, New York : Crabtree Publishing, [2019] |
  Series: Full STEAM ahead! | Includes index.
Identifiers: LCCN 2018058400 (print) | LCCN 2018059404 (ebook) |
  ISBN 9781427122537 (Electronic) |
  ISBN 9780778761877 (hardcover : alk. paper) |
  ISBN 9780778762348 (pbk. : alk. paper)
Subjects: LCSH: Day--Juvenile literature. | Night--Juvenile literature. | Earth (Planet)--Rotation--Juvenile literature. | Sun--Juvenile literature. | Moon--Juvenile literature.
Classification: LCC QB633 (ebook) | LCC QB633 .S545 2019 (print) | DDC 525/.35--dc23
LC record available at https://lccn.loc.gov/2018058400

Printed in the U.S.A./042019/CG20190215

Table of Contents

Crabtree Publishing Company
www.crabtreebooks.com   1-800-387-7650

Copyright © **2019 CRABTREE PUBLISHING COMPANY**. All rights reserved. No part of this publication may be reproduced, stored in a retrieval system or be transmitted in any form or by any means, electronic, mechanical, photocopying, recording, or otherwise, without the prior written permission of Crabtree Publishing Company. In Canada: We acknowledge the financial support of the Government of Canada through the Book Publishing Industry Development Program (BPIDP) for our publishing activities.

Published in Canada
Crabtree Publishing
616 Welland Ave.
St. Catharines, Ontario
L2M 5V6

Published in the United States
Crabtree Publishing
PMB 59051
350 Fifth Avenue, 59th Floor
New York, New York 10118

Published in the United Kingdom
Crabtree Publishing
Maritime House
Basin Road North, Hove
BN41 1WR

Published in Australia
Crabtree Publishing
Unit 3 – 5 Currumbin Court
Capalaba
QLD 4157

From Day to Night

Every day, the Sun lights the sky.
Every night, the Sun disappears.
The sky gets dark.

At night, we sometimes see the Moon.

← Moon

It is day, then night, then day again.
Day and night change in a cycle.

A cycle is something that happens again and again. It **repeats** in a pattern.

Earth Turns

Every 24 hours, Earth turns around one time. 24 hours make one day. Every day, our part of Earth turns toward the Sun, then away from the Sun. That makes day and night.

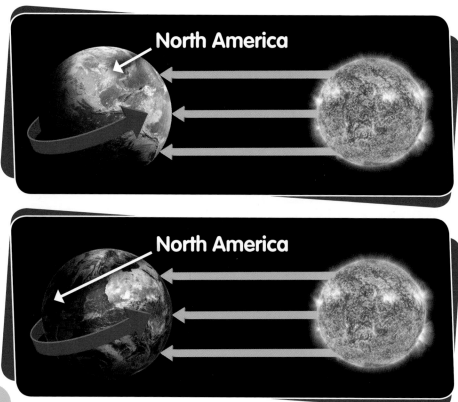

North America

It is day when our side of Earth is turned toward the Sun.

North America

It is night when our side of Earth is turned away from the Sun.

As Earth turns, the Sun seems to move across the sky.

sunrise

As our side of Earth turns to face the Sun, it looks like the Sun is **rising** in the sky. This is called sunrise.

noon

When our side of Earth fully faces the Sun, it is **noon**. The Sun looks like it is high in the sky.

sunset

As our side of Earth turns away from the Sun, it looks like the Sun is low in the sky. This is called sunset.

Observing Changes

The cycle of day to night is one pattern we can observe. To observe means to take in information using our **senses**.

hearing

smell

taste

sight

We have five senses. They are sight, hearing, smell, taste, and touch.

touch

We can use our sense of sight to observe changes in the sky. We can see the changes each morning, afternoon, evening, and night.

Never look directly at the Sun. It can damage your eyes.

Day Begins

A new day begins when the Sun rises. The Sun's **rays** light the sky.

As Earth turns, the side we live on turns toward the Sun. This makes the Sun look like it is rising in the sky.

In the morning, the Sun looks low in the sky. It is beginning to rise. It will look higher in the sky as the morning passes.

Look at the sky in the morning. Where is the Sun?

Afternoon

In the afternoon, the Sun looks like it has moved high up in the sky. It looks like it is right above us.

noon

At noon, our side of Earth fully faces the Sun. We see the Sun at the highest point in the sky.

shadow

When the Sun shines down on us, we see our shadow. Our shadow falls behind us when we face the Sun.

In the day, we may see clouds in the sky. We may see airplanes and birds flying above us. We might even see the Moon.

Day Ends

Evening follows afternoon. Our side of Earth is turning away from the Sun. The Sun looks low in the sky. It begins to disappear.

Sometimes, the sky looks red or pink at sunset.

In the evening, the clouds in the sky may look different than they did during the day. They may change color. They may change shape.

Night

It is night when our side of Earth has turned fully away from the Sun. The Sun seems to completely disappear. Without the Sun's rays to light the sky, it gets dark.

Instead of the Sun, you may see the Moon or stars in the night sky. You may see some clouds too. Sometimes, clouds cover everything in the night sky.

In the night sky, you might see different kinds of birds, or small animals called bats.

Airplanes that fly at night are lit up with flashing lights.

The Night Sky

When we look at the night sky, some things are farther away than others. Clouds are farther than birds. The Moon and stars are farther than clouds.

Stars are in the sky all the time. But we only see them in the dark night sky. In the day, the Sun makes the sky too bright to see stars.

Some things in the sky are too far away to see with our eyes. People can use special tools called **telescopes** to see them.

What Do You See?

The sky looks different as it changes from day to night.

We only see the Sun during the day. What else can we see only during the day?

We do not see the Sun at night. The sky is dark. We might see the Moon. What else can we see only at night?

You can observe how the sky changes.
Draw a **diagram** like the one shown here.
Look at the sky during the day and at night.
Write or draw the things you see.

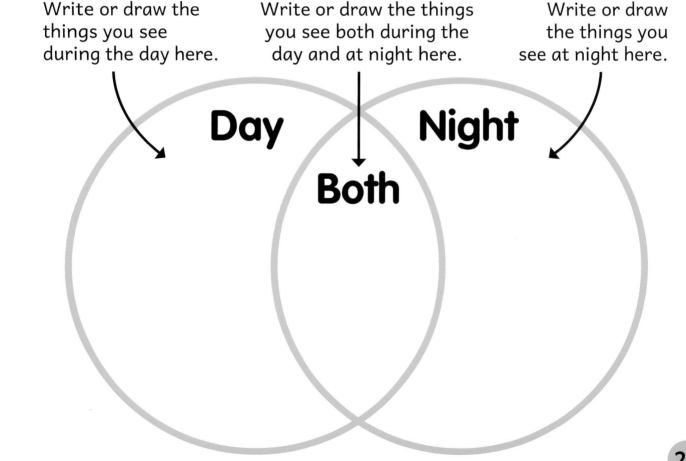

Write or draw the things you see during the day here.

Write or draw the things you see both during the day and at night here.

Write or draw the things you see at night here.

Day

Night

Both

Words to Know

diagram [DAHY-uh-gram] noun A drawing that shows the parts of an object or how it works

noon [noon] noun 12 o'clock p.m. in the day

rays [reys] noun Lines of light given off by bright objects

repeats [ri-PEETS] verb To do something again and again

rising [RAHY-zing] verb Moving upward

senses [sens-is] noun The ways that the body helps us understand the world around us, including sight, sound, hearing, taste, and touch

telescope [TEL-uh-skohp] noun A device that helps us see objects that are far away

A noun is a person, place, or thing.

A verb is an action word that tells you what someone or something does.

An adjective is a word that tells you what something is like.

Index

About the Author

Crystal Sikkens has been writing, editing, and providing photo research for Crabtree Publishing since 2001. She has helped produce hundreds of titles in various subjects. She most recently wrote two books for the popular Be An Engineer series.

To explore and learn more, enter the code at the Crabtree Plus website below.

www.crabtreeplus.com/fullsteamahead

Your code is:
fsa20

23

STEAM Notes for Educators

Full STEAM Ahead is a literacy series that helps readers build vocabulary, fluency, and comprehension while learning about big ideas in STEAM subjects. *Day and Night* uses strong diagrams and pictures with explanatory captions to help readers identify the information that can be found in visuals. The STEAM activity below helps readers extend the ideas in the book to build their skills in science, technology, and language arts.

Observing the Sun and Shadows

Children will be able to:
- Describe how Earth's rotation makes the Sun seem to move across the sky.
- Make predictions, observe, and reflect on how their shadow changes during one day.
- Use technology to document their observations, and present their findings.

Materials
- My Changing Shadow Worksheet
- Digital camera
- Chalk
- Large, concrete outdoor space, such as an empty parking lot

Guiding Prompts
After reading *Day and Night*, ask:
- Why does the Sun seem to move?
- What is a shadow? Have you seen your own? How are shadows related to the Sun?

Activity Prompts
Explain to children that we will observe our shadows to learn about Earth's rotation.
Pair children and hand out My Changing Shadow Worksheet. Review the worksheet with children. On a sunny day, guide children through activity:
1. In the morning, have children predict, on their worksheets, how their shadow will look.
2. Go outside to a large, concrete outdoor space. One child stands while the other uses chalk to trace their feet and their shadow. Label traced footprints. Switch children.
3. Measure and record information about the shadow on the worksheet.
4. Use a camera to take a photo of the shadow.
5. Repeat steps 1 to 4 at noon, and in the afternoon. Each time, child stands in same traced footprints.

Have children make an oral presentation. They should use the photos and describe their observations. Discuss the findings:
- Shadows change as the Sun changes position. When the Sun is low, our bodies block more sunlight and our shadows are longer. We see the opposite when the Sun is high.
- Remind children that the Sun only *seems* to change position because of Earth's rotation.

Extensions
- Invite children to make a model that demonstrates how shadows work.

To view and download the worksheet, visit **www.crabtreebooks.com/resources/ printables** or **www.crabtreeplus.com/ fullsteamahead** and enter the code **fsa20**.